EXP[illegible]NS

discove[illegible]y

by

Judith Fullard Smith

Booklet 10: a publication of

The Kindlers

In this series:

Journeying the Heartlands (2009)
Breakthrough to Unity (2010)
The Power we call God (2011)
Answering that of God (2012)
Love growing in Us (2012)
This I Warn you in Love (2013)
But who do you say that I am? (2013)
Signposts (2013)
Visioning New Fire (2013)
Explorations (2015)
Through us, not from us (2015)

Published in 2015 in the United Kingdom by *The Kindlers*, a project of North West London Area Quaker Meeting, Britain Yearly Meeting, of the Religious Society of Friends (Quakers).

ISBN: 978-0-9933627-0-5

Financed by the Joyce Green Association

For information about The Kindlers:
email: kindlers@quaker.org.uk

For information about Quakers in general:
www.quaker.org.uk tel. 0207 663 1000

Contents

Chapter one

Introduction

How it all began

This project, based on a small number of interviews with Quaker respondents, emerged out of another: running a "Writing the Spirit" group in my Local Meeting. The group still meets regularly and writes about a wide range of topics, but our early meetings focused on our spiritual autobiographies.

This work on spiritual storytelling started with a leading, which began stirring within me around the turn of the century, to come together with others to write about, reflect on and share our life stories and their most significant events and themes. Perhaps this was a slow-maturing response to the Woodbrooke Quaker Study Centre distance learning course of the late 1980s, *Gifts and Discoveries*, with its emphasis on our individual and communal stories. Certainly the leading grew clearer as I came upon other Quakers walking ahead of me on the same path. I came across Gillie Bolton's booklet, *Writing the Spirit* (published by Quaker Home Service 1994, now out of print), which gave me a framework for this group writing and sharing, and emphasised its spiritual basis. Later, reading Gil Skidmore's *Turning Inside Out*, and Alison Leonard's *Telling Our Stories* and *Living in Godless Times: Tales of Spiritual Travellers*, all concerned with spiritual autobiography, sharpened the focus of my original leading.

An article I wrote for the Quaker weekly publication *The Friend* (*Sharing our Stories*, published 24th September 2004) gave examples of our group's autobiographical writings, and emphasised the importance of the work, not only for ourselves, individually and as a group, but for those beyond it: such writings can be a means of both inreach, encouraging Friends in the Meeting as a whole to "seek to know one another in the things which are eternal" and also outreach, helping enquirers and newcomers to see how our journeys might relate to theirs. What is more, I feel that these stories of spiritual exploration could open ways forward for the more general spiritual search that is taking place: many people are feeling a sense of incompleteness and dissatisfaction with their lives and sometimes with the faith group in which they were brought up, while harbouring a growing sense that there is "something more".

And so the present project came gradually into being, as I sought to discover more about the stories already heard in the group, by conducting individual interviews with members of it, as well as with one or two other Friends in my Meeting. In addition, I have attempted, in my final chapter, to discover how this small group fits into the wider picture of contemporary spiritual exploration.

Because of many other commitments, there has been a delay of some years in producing this final version, though a number of amendments were made during the intervening period. Nevertheless, I hope these interviews will give a snapshot of early 21st-century spiritual exploration, and pave the way for fuller and more systematic study by others.

A final word, before we begin, about the distinction between "spiritual/spirituality" and "religion/religious." Those who call themselves "spiritual" often hasten to add that they are not religious. For them, the word "religion" now conjures up something institutional, official, public, social, with beliefs imposed upon us by those in authority; "spirituality" suggests something individual, often solitary, based in our own experience rather than what others have taught us, often hard to put into words, perhaps needing new words rather than the traditional ones. But we shall see later that there is often a desire for communal as well as individual spiritual experience.

My own story

Part of the excitement of hearing others' stories has been the shock of recognition, the realisation that I am not the spiritual outsider I once thought I was: others are journeying alongside me, exploring different paths but often coming back to the same road.

However I suppose I *was* unusual for my time and class in not having a religious upbringing. I was born in 1943 into a lower middle-class family, though with working-class grandparents. My parents were both teachers, but certainly not churchgoers: instead they were committed members of the Communist Party, at least until 1956, when they left the Party in protest at the Soviet invasion of Hungary. But they gave my brother and myself a happy and secure childhood, and many of their values have stayed with me and slotted easily into my Quaker life: belief in equality and respect for others, in family and friendship, in peace and international co-operation; and the environmental concerns they had in later life are now resonating more strongly with me.

So my first real encounter with religion was at primary school, and my first images of God and Jesus, discovered through Bible stories and hymns, were very conventional ones: I saw God as a kindly old man in the sky, and Jesus as the baby in the manger, or as "gentle Jesus" teaching, healing and rising from the dead. I was fortunate not to encounter the obsession with sin, judgement and punishment which a number of my friends have had to contend with at church or chapel.

But in my mid-teens I began to question it all. The death, from pneumonia, of a girl in my year at school brought the shocking realisation that someone of my own age could die, and suddenly death seemed very final, and my cosy ideas about the afterlife, and a loving God, very naïve. I was also becoming more aware of intolerant and hypocritical attitudes among a number of religious people I knew, expressing my indignation in some of the poems I was beginning to write. I subscribed to a humanist magazine and avidly read articles "proving" that Christianity wasn't true. Yet at the same time I was beginning to respond to Nature, and to the arts, particularly literature and music. A stay in France before university made me feel strongly the dark, mysterious quality of Roman Catholic churches, and the atmosphere of worship within them. I even felt the beginnings of an interest in Quakerism, for instance when my school's deputy head, who was a Friend, gave a talk on Quakers and Quaker worship.

My student days began to set me on a new spiritual path. I encountered evangelical religion and developed my interest in humanism, but decided before long that neither was for me, both in a sense too narrowly dogmatic and neither true to my own experience. Fortunately, however, there were also lectures offering "Objections to Christianity" by the university's theologians, and discussions deep into the night with my small group of friends. I also read John Robinson's *Honest to God*, with its view of God as "the ground of our being", which made more sense to me than picturing the "old man in the sky". Further visits to France confirmed my earlier spiritual stirrings. The seed was sown, the scene set.

But for some years I took it no further. Much of my first year as a research student was bleak and lonely, a "dark night of the soul", when life seemed absurd and meaningless, religion irrelevant to what I was going through. When I finally began work as a lecturer, life became busy and exciting, with colleagues, students, a new way of life to get to know. Spiritual concerns and questions became irrelevant in a different way, pushed into the background, only occasionally re-awakened by apparently chance incidents, conversations or moments of reflection.

It was through meeting my future husband, Martin, when both of us were in our late twenties, that religion began to come more to the fore again. We both felt there was more to life than wealth and success, and both reacted against some aspects of religion while feeling the call of the spiritual both within and outside it.

Marriage, a move to a smaller town, and particularly motherhood, followed later by new part-time work with the Open University, all brought changes and challenges which left little room for spiritual exploration. However, starting a family did give us both the nagging feeling that we wanted our children to have a spiritual dimension in their lives. My occasional encounters with Quakerism and Quakers finally (after the arrival of our second child) led me to write a very hesitant response to a newspaper advert about Friends, pointing out that I was, if anything, an agnostic and unsure whether I was proper Quaker material! George Gorman replied encouragingly and sent his book, *Introducing Quakers*. There were also details of our nearest Meeting House, and on a cold January day in 1978 I finally plucked up courage to attend, and was met by a warm welcome, immediately feeling at home in a silence whose extraordinary quality I later described as "a silence I can almost touch", broken only by two short and simple pieces of ministry, as I later found they were called.

We gradually built up a relationship with this small and friendly Meeting, and perhaps in those early days had rather a rosy view of Quakerism. But some twenty one months after my first Meeting for Worship, it was "all change" again, with a new job, in a large city, for Martin, a new home in a very different place, and, before long, the arrival of our third child. It took some years, too, for me to be settled in part-time work, particularly, again, with the Open University, and also in adult continuing education, which felt right for me.

We also had to get used to a new Meeting, and began to see the problems as well as the pleasures of being a Quaker. With only a few really active members, there was often a preoccupation with the "jobs" that needed doing, with the letter rather than the spirit. Silence in Meetings for Worship could seem empty and lifeless at times, business meetings could be flat and dull, or with tensions and conflict at or below the surface. Yet our twenty years in this Meeting also brought us the best of Quakerism, with some Meetings suddenly sparking to life through inspired ministry, with the deep spiritual exploration and fellowship offered by the *Gifts and Discoveries* distance learning course, and with Monthly Meeting conferences in the Lakes and in Shropshire. And there were always Friends – including Martin – who "let [their lives] speak", whether in quietly doing good among Ffriends and neighbours, trying to respond to the crises, such as unemployment, that hit the city, or bringing greater depth to our worship. Often, though, during this busy period in our lives, with many work and family commitments, spiritual exploration seemed a rare luxury.

It was in the next phase of our lives – too active to be called "retirement" – after we moved to a small country town in a beautiful setting, that it proved possible to bring spiritual exploration centre stage. It seemed to take myriad forms for me, some shared with Martin: deep Sunday worship in our old eighteenth century Meeting House; midweek worship, followed by discussion, and writing and healing group meetings held there; participating in and helping to facilitate retreats, Quiet Days and similar events; attending Experiment with Light (a guided meditation based on the writings of early Friends) meetings in a nearby, even older, Meeting House. There have been opportunities, too, to explore new interpretations of the Christian faith in a small local retreat house, to take part in ecumenical or interfaith gatherings; and to take walks in the hills and valleys near here, or simply sit quietly in the early morning reading, journalling and looking out at the view.

This spiritual feast has, however, been accompanied by everyday worries and chores (still including too many Quaker ones), and a growing awareness that we were ageing, perhaps approaching our last years. But this has only made each day more precious, and given our spiritual exploration still more depth, particularly in the two extra years Martin was given. After being resuscitated following a cardiac arrest, and undergoing heart bypass surgery, he has been able to carry out more of what he felt called to do, and we have both treasured each day even more. He died very suddenly in January 2015 while out cycling with friends, a great loss to his family and friends, but leaving us the legacy of his love and inspiration.

Now I am left with a still stronger sense of connection with a "spirit that…rolls through all things" as I first heard it called by Wordsworth (in *Lines composed above Tintern Abbey*) some fifty five years ago. This is a spirit which is present in all life, in all experience if we are open to it, somehow both intimately known and deeply mysterious, which connects us in love to all human beings and all creation. I have the feeling, though I can't prove it, that all spiritual experience is essentially one, though expressed in many different words and actions. But let us hear what other spiritual explorers have to say.

An introduction to the interviewees

This is a group of eleven people. Nine of them were involved in the writing group at the time of the original interviews, and three of them still take part in it. The other two, like nearly all the rest of the group, have had connections with my Local Meeting. I did not interview one of these, Paul, but had permission from him to quote from the article on his spiritual journey which he wrote for our Meeting newsletter. The group have had a varied experience of Quakerism, and at least one of them dislikes the label "Quaker" or indeed any other religious label. Most are "jigsaw people", to use Eleanor Nesbitt's description (*Friends Quarterly*, Issue One 2009,

"Quakerism and other faiths", p.20): they have had (or still have) other spiritual allegiances besides their Quaker connections. Since some time has elapsed between the initial interviews and this final draft, I have, wherever possible, checked that those who took part are happy with what I have written, and have included updates on their spiritual journeys, gleaned in conversation, by e-mail or telephone, where interviewees felt they wanted to add these.

A brief introduction to the individual members of the group may be helpful. All are, or have been, married. **Graham** has two grown-up children and has recently become a grandfather. He took early retirement from university lecturing and for some years has worked as a cycling trainer. **Dave**, another retired university lecturer, is a friend and former colleague of Graham's, through whom he heard about the writing group, as he does not live locally. He also has two adult children and also took early retirement, in his case because he has ME. **Gwynneth** is a widow and great-grandmother, formerly a nurse. **Janet**, who has a son and two granddaughters, was for many years a schoolteacher before becoming an Alexander Technique teacher. **Jan**, also a grandmother, married her second husband in our Meeting House, and before retirement did administrative work for a painting and decorating company. She and her husband went to live in France a few years ago, but Jan felt very isolated there and has returned to England and our area. **Kevin** and **Michelle** are husband and wife and have an adult foster-daughter, now married with two children. They are former probation officers who became university lecturers, teaching courses for probation officers and later police officers; both are now retired. **Sue** has a student son and works in mental health in both hospital and community settings. **Wendy**, a lifelong Methodist, is married to a birthright member of our Meeting. She currently does voluntary work, and previously worked in shops, particularly pharmacies. **David**, who died in December 2011, never attended the writing group. He was a widower with no children of his own, but had close ties with his "adopted" family, former neighbours of his. His early career as an opera singer was followed by many years as a lecturer in singing. **Paul**, who has a son in his twenties, used to work for the probation service before training to teach. He now works as a school cover supervisor and has recently trained as a yoga teacher.

For reflection and sharing

- **How might you set up a group to share your spiritual journeys in your own Local Meeting or other Quaker group?**
- **What particular landmarks or turning points can you see in your own spiritual journey?**

Chapter two

The Outer Journey: Other Faith Groups

I shall begin with the group's childhood spiritual experiences, which are perhaps less diverse than their later ones. Then I shall look at each of their varied outer journeys in turn, firstly with non-Quaker groups.

Early experiences

Only one respondent, Paul, had had no family or church background as a child, and was put off, rather than attracted by his experience of worship at school: "I quickly developed a dislike and distrust for organised worship… My spiritual instincts found nothing to feed on but plenty to chafe against." A number of the other respondents attended church and/or Sunday school but their parents did not go to church. These tended to be unimpressed: "It didn't mean anything to me" (Gwynneth); "A lot of it didn't touch me" (Dave). David "[didn't] remember questioning" the Methodist Sunday school to which he was sent, and enjoyed activities like doing a shadow play. Those who had a churchgoing parent or parents tended to take religion for granted: "part of the wallpaper" (Kevin); "it was taken for granted that Sunday was church day" (Wendy). For Graham, it was "almost a tribal thing": with very few exceptions his fellow-villagers were either Anglican or Methodist.

For some, there were traditional images of God which they soon left behind them. "They threatened us (Gwynneth and other children she knew) with God" – they were told that God could see everything, though they didn't believe it. Graham saw God as "a bearded old gentleman on a cloud" as portrayed in the stained-glass windows, "kindly" but also "punitive…prepared to wield the big stick if necessary." Aspects of childhood religion still remain with a number of respondents, however: Bible stories were fondly remembered by several, particular hymns by one or two, and there were memories of the aesthetic or dramatic appeal of church or worship: "the colours of the windows and the sense of size and space" in the church (Janet); and the drama of Catholic ritual and worship: vestments, candles, stained glass, the incense flaring up as it was thrown into the charcoal (Kevin).

A deep relationship with the divine or sense of the spiritual was rare in childhood, though several had early glimmerings of it. Wendy has retained her early image of God: "there is somebody there who protects us and looks after us", and Sue was "quite pious", going into church to pray on the way home from school, and regularly to Choral Evensong from about the age of ten, going on to be "quite evangelical" in her early teens. Jan felt closeness to a "loving Other" through certain hymns when a child member of her church choir. And, for two respondents, deep spiritual experience came through Nature. Gwynneth remembers the wonder of the masses of bluebells when she was taken for a walk as a small child, and she had many similar experiences among the "fields and footpaths" in the country where she lived and played with her brothers and sisters. Paul describes in detail a particular experience when he was about ten and "skipping school", sitting in the autumn sunlight in an orchard, and his sense of awe, which is difficult to describe adequately in words: "At best I can only say I felt a connection with something so deep and satisfying that the moment took on a dreamlike quality, only all my senses were sharpened rather than dulled. Life suddenly had a potential for a deeper interest and satisfaction, the pursuit of which became my spiritual quest".

And, for several of the respondents, whatever their later beliefs, this early religious upbringing has remained deeply embedded in their consciousness: a "thorough induction", "a benchmark, a reference point" (Graham); for Sue, "well-versed in the liturgy of the Church" from an early age, it has become "second nature". Wendy summed it up like this: "If you've had some sort of religious upbringing, it stays with you through life; whether you follow that path or not, it's there at the back of your mind, in the depths of your brain somewhere."

Yet, while Wendy stayed on, feeling only slightly rebellious, for most, their teenage years brought questioning or simply drifting away.

Journeying onward

Both Wendy and Michelle have remained for most of their lives with one particular group. After attending an Anglican Sunday school as a child, **Michelle** gave up going to church even before she reached her teens, when she failed to get proper answers to the questions she was asking. Soon afterwards she discovered Quakers, with whom she has had a strong, but sometimes difficult, "on-off" relationship (see **Chapter Three,** *Quaker Experience*).

Wendy feels her "roots" are in Methodism. She had a strong Methodist upbringing and her father was a lay preacher. She expects to stay there as she has always done, with the exception of a period in her twenties when she tried other churches, notably an evangelical one. When she met her future husband, she went back to Methodism as a secure background to the changes in her life. It was difficult for her to get used to a new Methodist church when she moved to one on marriage, but after a time she felt more accepted and involved. She attends a Free Methodist Church, where the members sometimes lead a service and she "enjoys the challenge" of doing this.

Others had no particular religious ties, once they left their birth religion behind, until they came to Friends. **Kevin**, for instance, moved away from the Catholic Church in which he had been brought up and had served as an altar boy. He, like Michelle, felt dissatisfied with the priests' attempts to answer his questions. He had no formal experience of religion after his late teens, until, through Michelle, he came to Friends in his thirties.

In his teens, **Graham** had felt strong peer pressure, critical and mocking of religion, though for a time continued to attend church without his friends' knowledge. However he drifted away from it when he became involved in left-wing politics at university; and though, through walking and cycling, he had experienced the intense response to the natural world which Gwynneth and Paul had felt as children, he did not then connect it with the God of his childhood. By his early twenties he felt he had "certainly rejected formal religion", but by the time he met his future wife had "swung back to the notion of a belief in God", seeing himself as a "Christian believer but I wasn't going to church", and therefore felt he would not be true to himself if he married in church. However he felt it right for his two children to be baptised: "I felt I'd like them to have a start in this faith", as he had valued his own introduction to it. From then on for many years he was very committed to both work and family, and formal religion had no place in his life. His sense of awe and connection in the presence of Nature continued, but his spiritual search did not really develop until he was in his forties.

Several respondents continued, after a shorter time away, to explore different faith groups, some mainly within Christianity, others venturing further afield.

Despite her early piety, **Sue** had become "quite frustrated" with religion by the time she was in the Lower Sixth, "doing all sorts of gymnastics and acrobatics to make it make sense." However, she found herself still involved in Anglican circles when at university, where her uncle was the very radical college chaplain. She joined the Anglican Society and discovered the "linking of religious thought with aesthetics" at the High Anglican Church she attended, with its beautiful architecture and music and its "great speakers". But she was becoming more "circumspect" about her faith, not wanting to be "labelled", even for a time moving away from religion, and later joining the Sea of Faith Network. The debate over the ordination of women, and the subsequent "outpouring of vitriol" after women were admitted to the priesthood, finally drove her away from the Anglican Church, though much in its language and liturgy is still close to her heart. The atmosphere of a church when there are "no set services" (though she still loves Christmas ones), or there is a "completely separate deal" like attendance at Choral Evensong, is still important to her.

Dave had moved away from formal religion. From his early teens he experienced the "nagging thought" that "it can't be that just Christians are the good guys and the rest are the bad guys. It can't be that simple." For much of his life he has had a stronger commitment to politics than to religion: like Graham, he was actively involved in left-of-centre politics as a young man, and later for many years was very committed to a disability rights organisation at both regional and national levels. Nevertheless he, again like Graham, found spiritual awareness as he cycled and walked in the country. Soon after his first child's birth, he started attending an Anglican church again, and was confirmed in his early thirties: "I almost became quite fervent at one point". But he eventually moved away when there were questioning, even hostile, reactions to the yoga classes he and his wife attended, and a refusal to accept, at a Bible study group, that there might be alternative interpretations of the passage they were discussing. Increasingly he felt those earlier suspicious of fundamentalist, evangelical attitudes – "My way's right, your way's wrong" – again concluding that "life isn't that simple", and he has "retained that [view] to this day".

He feels the Nonconformist churches, like the Quakers, have at least favoured "more equality, less hierarchy" than the established Church, and this he finds "more healthy". Indeed, he attended a local Methodist church for "a good couple of years" after leaving the Anglican one. Both congregation and minister there were good people, "but it just didn't provide what I was looking for" – and a much later foray into Methodism again left him dissatisfied eventually, despite finding much to admire. No church really "spoke to my condition" (including a later encounter with Roman Catholicism, when he stood godparent to a Catholic child, though it did remind him of the High Anglican church of his upbringing). He was a non-churchgoer for about a dozen years, but continued and still continues to admire individuals or groups who live out their faith, like members of the Salvation Army, who are really "on the front line". For several years in the 1990s he worked in Ethiopia, which gave him a different perspective. The Ethiopians' very old version of Christianity (going back to about 560 CE) gives more emphasis to the Old Testament and has links with Judaism. There, every small village has both a church and a mosque, and Dave feels the mutual toleration of Christianity and Islam is something we can learn from: each religion "has equal respect for the other." At different times in his life, he has read books about both Islam and Judaism, finding both make sense to him.

Jan became engaged to a Roman Catholic in her late teens, had preparatory meetings with the local priest, and felt attracted to the Church's structure and ritual. The couple were married in 1963, around the time of Vatican II, and masses were held in English from then on. Her husband was unhappy with this and stopped attending church, but Jan continued, still feeling drawn to the ritual – the incense, music and so on – which felt like "getting closer to God." The many holy days of obligation, when attendance at mass was obligatory, were difficult to keep to, but she "wanted to be religious" and felt giving up things was important. Both her daughters were baptised into the Catholic Church and attended Catholic schools.

When the family moved to this area in the late 1970s, she became more of an explorer, at first attending a High Anglican church as the Catholic one was some distance away. A little later, as well as occasionally attending Quaker Meetings, she did a lot of reading about Eastern religions. Then, through one of her daughters, she became involved with the Christadelphians: both were baptised on the same day in 1987. Sometimes she felt she had "touched something important" here, and she valued Bible study sessions, but she had difficulties with the Christadelphians' strict fundamentalist and narrowly moralistic attitudes. At a particularly low point in her life some time later, a friend suggested she try the United Churches healing ministry. Here she received counselling, and felt a connection between belief and everyday life, though the "happy clappy" services did not appeal to her. At times she felt she was "swinging between high ritual, middle-way Anglicanism and total atheism", but she was gradually beginning to find her own way through developing her own spiritual practices. After some time in our Meeting, she felt drawn to the Jehovah's Witnesses and stayed with them for about three years before returning to us, not having found the deep fellowship and spirituality she had hoped for, nor the engagement with everyday life, and feeling the demands the group made on her could wreck her marriage. But she still respects the Witnesses' deep knowledge of the Bible.

Others have eventually gone on to explore different faiths and philosophies. **Gwynneth** lingered awhile in her local church in her teens, but mainly because she could play badminton in the church hall if she attended church. After moving away from home to train as a nurse, she began a long but often unsatisfying association with mainstream religion before her spiritual life really flowered in less orthodox ways in her later years. During her student days she attended a Roman Catholic church with a Catholic fellow-student. It appealed to her because her friend was so happy in her religion and the priest was a very good man; but she didn't think much of services in Latin, or the confessional, or all those "You must's." After training and working as a midwife, she married an Anglican curate and the couple lived for a time in Wales, then moved to this area, where she still lives. While she liked the services, especially Holy Communion, she found a great deal was expected of her as a vicar's wife, struggled with reading the Bible, and disliked the "Do as I say but not as I do" attitude of some church members. After nearly twenty years the marriage ended and she became disillusioned with the Church and stopped attending, no longer having "faith in praying", though still accepting "the underlying belief".

Her second marriage was a very happy one, but life was very busy, with little room for spirituality, though they tried at least to "do to others as we would have them do to us." After her husband's sudden death, she became "a hermit" for a while, at last venturing out and beginning to develop the spiritual dimension of her life through adult education classes in "relaxation and stress control", in healing, and later in counselling classes, based on an open sharing of feelings. After sampling philosophy classes, which turned out to be a cover for some kind of cult, secretive and authoritarian, she had a better experience with a wisdom teachings course, taken from a number of traditions, giving "knowledge" and "consolation", "clearing the mind".

And from 1992 for a number of years she would go to the Findhorn Community for week-long workshops on particular themes. Being part of a community, even temporarily, gave "hope", "something else to think about." She enjoyed learning practical outdoor skills and being led into meditation through "inner listening": holding a stone, offering up a problem and waiting for an answer, which might come immediately or much later, and might not necessarily be the one desired or expected.

At the time of the interview she was still an avid reader of books offering spiritual enlightenment, though reading did at times give her "mental indigestion", making everything seem "contradictory." In recent years eyesight problems have made reading more difficult for her.

David encountered both Quakerism and Buddhism in middle age, but until his early forties he was a Christian Scientist, having begun to attend their Sunday school in his later childhood when his mother became friendly with neighbours who were Christian Scientists. In his earlier days there it was quite a fashionable religion – with services and particularly the Wednesday evening "testimony meetings" always crowded – "quiet and dignified", attracting many middle-class, educated people. But he found it too inflexible for him ("I've never had a very obedient mentality"), with rigid rules, very much a "religion of the book"*(Science and Health)*, and in his later years there it became ever more "inward-looking", which was "part of its downfall". Numbers were falling, and the Church's fortunes were not revived by what, to his mind, was an ill-advised "makeover", commissioned from an advertising firm by its directors in the USA. He also disagreed with Christian Science's promotion of "radical reliance": the "notorious" refusal of medical treatment, "virtually as an article of faith, and often with fatal consequences". His wife and mother both tragically died as a result of this, though at the time of his resignation it was the authoritarian nature of the church government which made him particularly unhappy. However, he continued to value its moments of "spiritual insight", its "very lofty but not personal" concept of God, seen in the church's founder Mary Baker Eddy's "seven synonyms for God".

He had begun to attend Friends' Meetings while still living in London, and continued to do so when he and his wife moved to this area. It was after another move some years later that he began to attend a Buddhist group with an excellent lay (later ordained) teacher whose teaching he found "immensely beneficial", and he continued to attend there after moving back to our area. The community expanded and set up other centres, so that David was eventually able to attend sessions nearer his home, though with less benefit: he found the teachers less skilled and experienced. He then encountered a book by a Tibetan monk, *The Tibetan Book of Living and Dying*, and was able to attend his classes and those of other monks in London from time to time, as well as two three-day sessions of teachings by the Dalai Lama, which were "enormously impressive." But locally he "felt a bit adrift in a way" not having "a spiritual community", and decided to go back to his local Meeting. After a time, however, he also returned to another Buddhist group in his nearest town: "I like to be taught." This he found "a lovely community", well looked after by a "very loving" Indian nun who did most of the teaching. At the time of the interview he went there only rarely, as he couldn't hear the nun very well, but he liked to study ancient texts with her commentary. Buddhism remained important to him: it could seem inflexible, but he felt it was "pretty realistic", with "no fantasies", no "tricks of salvation."

Janet's spiritual journey has taken her far away from traditional Christianity. She was able to attend a Quaker boarding-school through a scheme run by her local council, and aspects of Quakerism remained in the background during her later spiritual explorations, prompting her eventually to return to Friends.

In her late teens, she had a period of "extreme despair" as she struggled to answer questions like "What's it all about?" and "Why are we here?" Then, while at teacher training college, she discovered the teachings of Gurdjieff and gave up her studies (though later completing them and becoming a teacher) in order to learn more about them. She was impressed from the outset by the "thoughtful", "considered" approach of those giving the teachings: they were "speaking from the heart", "from their own experiences" rather as in Meeting for Worship. And they were not dogmatic and didn't mention God (which would have put her off at that time), but what they said seemed to her to be "pure commonsense", answering the despairing questions she had been asking a year or two earlier. Gurdjieff saw the majority of people as behaving like "mad machines", on "automatic pilot": they needed to seek to understand themselves before they could look outwards, to be aware, present to themselves and the present moment, and to know the different "centres" in each of us, based in the intellect, the emotions, and the body and its movements. Janet gradually discovered how Gurdjieff's teachings used different activities to develop these different centres: the teaching and questioning developed the intellectual centre, but there were also movement sequences based on monastic and dervish traditions, and "the work", practical group-based activities. All enabled the different centres to "be in communication and in harmony", with the inner knowledge reflected out into the world. Janet became very involved with Gurdjieff groups: the teachings and activities became "the focus of my life" for a period of about fifteen years.

Eventually she left the groups, feeling that they had taken over too much of her life, though Gurdjieff's ideas remained "very much ingrained in my way of operating and thinking", and she returned to them from time to time. Having tried church attendance for a time, she became "an erratic attender" at her present Quaker Meeting. Yet she felt she needed more "guidance" and "structure" than Quakers were providing, and, like David, began attending classes on Buddhist teachings and practices. "It fitted in pretty comfortably with my own picture of life" and Gurdjieff's teachings. She was very involved in the setting up of a Tibetan Buddhist Centre in her local area, but came to feel there was too much ritual, a certain "rigidity" about the teachings, especially as, in her view as in David's, the teachers were often young and inexperienced. She finally left (though she still attends occasionally), and gradually began attending Meeting more: "Everything's compatible at the root", she feels, and now sees her "personal path as a bit of a mesh of all these different ingredients", a "mish-mash", but with much more coming together of the different elements as time goes on.

For **Paul**, formal religion played little part in his life before he came to Friends. We have noted that he found his first experiences of worship, in school, stifling and joyless. After his first real spiritual experience in the "October orchard", he sought similar experiences, not only in Nature, but also in church, and persuaded friends to take him along to their church services. One visit to the Jehovah's Witnesses was enough; but he attended Catholic Mass a number of times, enjoying its atmosphere and drama: "the sense of dramatic dark ages and suffering", but "I had no sense of drawing close to the feelings I was seeking." For a while, "my spiritual side was abandoned" as he became preoccupied with the opposite sex and Heavy Metal music.

Then in his late teens a relationship with an older woman introduced him to "the exciting moonlit world of paganism", an involvement which was to last ten years, the last two bringing him into contact with Wicca. He enjoyed the magic, mystery and fun, as well as the lack of "any officious intermediary getting in my way", and "this nature-based religion" seemed to be the right one for him, given his affinity with the natural world, providing him with a "belief structure", "an acceptable explanation for our relationships with the spiritual world." Eventually, however, he realised that this was a "spiritual life" that "had form", but "no substance", none of the depth of his first spiritual experience, and moreover that its structure still included "leaders and followers" and "had returned me to that place where one is preached at that had been so uncomfortable before." He felt he had to leave the group, and unsuccessfully tried to fill the spiritual void with green politics and anarchism. But he knew intuitively that "the systems we create politically are just surface noises on a deeper human truth" and before long restarted the spiritual search which eventually brought him to Quakerism.

For reflection and sharing

- **To what other groups have your spiritual explorations taken you before – or since – you discovered Quakerism?**
- **Which aspects of these have you been happy to leave behind, and which do you still value?**

Chapter three

The Outer Journey: Quaker Experience

For most of the respondents, their discovery of Friends, and movement to a greater – sometimes lesser – commitment, was a gradual, intermittent process, beginning for many of them through actually meeting Friends, most obviously in the cases of Kevin and Wendy, whose respective partners were and still are Quakers. When Wendy first met her future husband, she knew little about Quakers, and thought of them as some "strange sect", but was reassured by her father's comment that if her new friend was a Quaker, "he's a good man." Kevin had known Michelle for several years, and talked to her a lot about Quakerism, before deciding he would like to try Meeting for Worship for himself.

Michelle herself had heard a talk about Quakers at school when she was twelve or thirteen, and she and a schoolfriend decided to go to a Quaker Meeting in their locality. Janet, as we have seen, also encountered Quakers early, through her time at a Quaker boarding-school, and grew to value Friends' tolerant attitudes, and the "Quaker quiet", often to the extent of escaping to walk in its gardens on her own instead of going to the formal school Meeting for Worship. This quiet was to draw her back many years later. Sue met a number of Friends when she joined the Sea of Faith Network and, in her growing disillusionment with the Anglican Church, and search for a spiritual home, decided it was "better to go somewhere where people think like this to start with", and was ready to try Friends. The first Quakers Paul met were the parents of a close friend, and made a profound impression on him: "The peaceful way they conducted their lives and their warmth towards me was inspiring."

For others that first contact was with a Meeting for Worship or a Meeting House, encountered as if by chance, though in all these cases there was probably some latent interest or curiosity. Gwynneth lived near our Meeting House and decided to come and see the place for herself on a Heritage Open Day; Jan met someone who was friendly with a Quaker from a local Meeting and occasionally went to Meeting with them; David decided he would like to attend the wedding of a friend of a friend at Friends House.

The written and broadcast word also played its part. After her first encounters with Quakers, Sue sent for Quaker literature and received Harvey Gillman's *A Light that is Shining*; Dave was impressed – and continues to be impressed – by what he read and heard of the courage and integrity of early Friends, of Quaker reformers and conscientious objectors, and had a "high regard" for Gerald Priestland, through his broadcasts, before finding out he was a Quaker and coming across his account of his own discovery of Friends, *Coming Home.* This was the "final trigger": Dave too sent off for Quaker literature through the post. David picked up *Advices and Queries*, probably at the Quaker wedding he attended, and was "very, very impressed". From then on, the book "never stayed in a drawer". He consulted it regularly and found it "pretty unbeatable." Graham made a conscious effort, once he realised what was missing in his life, to read up about other faiths and faith groups: his decision to try Friends was a rational one – as he said, almost "a consumer choice" – because it was "anchored in something that I knew". "The Quaker faith", he added, "seemed to have that openness and acceptance of difference, but nevertheless a strong identification with key principles that I felt important."

For some, Meeting for Worship seemed strange at first. Kevin was "quite mesmerised by the contrast with Roman Catholicism"; Wendy found it strange too at the first couple of Meetings she went to, and feels that "people need to go to at least two or three" before they can decide whether it is for them or not. She initially found the Friends there "a strange, odd bunch of people." David found he couldn't "settle down" to Quaker Meetings for a time, and thought Quakerism wasn't for him, but eventually found a Meeting which worked for him. Others felt immediately at home: "from day one", said Sue. For many, Meeting for Worship at once, or very soon, made a great impact on them, with the quality of its silence particularly mentioned. Sue, at that first Meeting, felt happy with the silence, and the three or four pieces of ministry appealed to her in the way that they all "seemed to resonate off one another." Graham described the silence of Meeting for Worship as "powerful beyond anything that I'd experienced before" and was "very moved by it", becoming "a great ambassador for silence". Despite the unfamiliarity of the experience, Kevin also responded to "the strange quality and depth of the silence" and found the ministry a "revelation" in its "ordinariness", "sharing rather than preaching". Wendy "enjoyed the quietness" and felt there was a "presence" in her husband's Meeting.

The welcoming attitude of Friends was also noticed on those first visits. After arriving very late following a long bus journey to her first Meeting, Michelle and her friend were found "lurking in the hallway" and welcomed. Sue at her first Meeting found the added bonus of something she had not expected to have, communal support ("I'd ploughed my own religious furrow" for so long). She "blurted out" that she was an "angry Anglican" and got the response, "We're all angry Anglicans here." At the first few Meetings she attended, Jan felt comforted, not only by "the simple setting and the silence", but also by the "genuine warmth" of the people she met there.

Two of the respondents have settled into a pattern of occasional attendance only. After attending Meeting for Worship several times, **Gwynneth** feels no particular desire to return, but "I'm still here", and she still feels a link with the Meeting. She has occasionally come to midweek discussion meetings, and regularly attended the writing group for a while. **Wendy's** attendances at Meeting for Worship are rare now that she has more responsibilities in her own church, though until recently she has participated regularly in the writing group, and has found that both sit quite comfortably with her Methodism. She feels that "you're never too old to learn from other people", that you "just have to accept" that everyone in the Meeting is different, and that all have "very different opinions – that makes up the whole." Meeting for Worship itself, she thinks, "does you good", it's "quite relaxing", it "pulls you up a little bit", as it isn't as "busy" as other forms of worship, with people "jumping up and down." She was "scared" the first time she spoke in Meeting, partly because she "felt people wouldn't accept it", but after the first couple of times "it didn't bother me". She spoke "if I feel led" to minister. She would find her "hands go hot" and wouldn't want to speak that day, but "it's a compulsion."

Jan attended our Meeting quite frequently from early 2005, and we have noted that she and her second husband were married at our Meeting House (in April 2005); also that she returned to us after about three years with the Jehovah's Witnesses, though she had still continued to attend the writing group during her time away. She was just settling into the Meeting again when she and her husband made their decision to go and live in France. Not long after arriving there, she wrote that there were few choices spiritually. She found Mass rather "impersonal", and there were no Quaker Meetings anywhere in her area. But she found that prayer "is of special value in this situation", and was glad to have the copy of *Quaker Faith and Practice* we had given her. She was happy, too, to have found a local choir where she could share again in "the universal language of music" even though French didn't yet come easily to her. However, as also mentioned earlier, she did not settle in France, has returned to our area, and she has now begun attending the writing group again sometimes.

Others have had a longer and/or more complicated connection with Friends, and it has to be said that for quite a while **David**, despite age and health problems, was the only one of the group who still attended our Meeting regularly. Even after moving to sheltered accommodation in a nearby town, and trying to attend other Local Meetings, he returned to us eventually, seeing our Meeting as his spiritual home. Even for him, the Quaker path has not been entirely smooth. We have seen that, though *Advices and Queries* soon became and remained a constant companion and guide, it was some time before he found a Meeting that suited him. Later he and his wife moved north and he found a home in another Meeting, where he eventually became Clerk. He then began attending our Meeting before another move brought him a less than happy experience of Quakerism, including some "humanist" ministry. It was at this point that he became involved with Buddhism. Some years later, when back in this area, and having a less satisfactory connection with Buddhism locally, he felt the need of a "sangha", a community, and found it again in our Meeting. There he was welcomed as if he had been absent for a matter of weeks rather than years, and he "never really looked back." Though he would have liked more use of both *Advices and Queries* and *Quaker Faith and Practice*, more of the teaching which he found in Buddhism, David felt that Friends were of most importance in his life, the "most rock-like thing". He greatly valued the influence of individual Friends, of our Meeting, and of the Society in general, as well as the outlook embodied in *Advices and Queries* and in the Testimonies, particularly, for him, the Peace Testimony. He asserted that "Racism has no place in the Quaker outlook", that Quakers accept "people with all sorts of problems", and summed it all up by praising "the openness and acceptance of Friends."

At the time of the original interview survey, **Paul** wrote very enthusiastically about his Quaker experience. He had attended our Meeting for several years and became a member in 2002. "I soaked up my first year of Quaker Meetings like a sponge. Over the last three years I've had no blinding visions. I've had no sudden insights or revelations, but with each Meeting my awareness of my spiritual self has progressed.

With that awareness is developing a gentle connection with that divine reality which I believe is present behind everything. I find it just below the surface and behind the noise I make when I try to explain things or make things happen. Little by little it is not the moment but the whole of my life that is becoming inspired."

In those earlier years with us, he "found some real peace in Meetings", and valued above all "the freedom of Quakers to find spiritual inspiration where they may". In more recent years, however, he has rarely come to Meeting, finding it "less rewarding than walks up in the hills or my 'as and when' meditations ar home." He has been finding Quakerism "insubstantial", lacking solidity, perhaps because he doesn't have "a strong foothold in Christianity" despite being "quite a fan" of Jesus' teachings. For a time, he felt Buddhism had that solidity, but even when his interest in it waned and Quakerism began to beckon again, he felt that he would feel freer, happier and less guilty as an attender than as a member. Eventually he did indeed resign his membership, continuing to attend very occasionally.

In **Graham's** original interview there was perhaps a sense that his early enthusiasm had cooled a little. The silence of Meeting for Worship had "less impact" for him, and he didn't find in it that initial intense spiritual experience. However, he still felt that "our lives are too cluttered, noisy and interrupted", that we don't get any chance to step outside of that and reflect in a quiet meditative way: silence can be very much "a way into some kind of spiritual experience". And he still had "a strong need to go" to Meeting for Worship: "it means a lot to me", and now had more to do with a kind of "spiritual sharing"; it was "spiritually refreshing." He also valued the openness and "flexibility" of Quakerism, feeling that it gave him "a scope for movement in a spiritual arena that I find very healthy". It was "respecting of individuals within it rather than the clergy or the system", though he conceded that there is a certain formality about Meeting for Worship, and that Quakerism still has rules, but less overt ones than some other faith groups. He valued, too, the Quaker principle of "answering that of God in every one", treating others with respect, doing what one can to make life better and more enriching, not in a merely humanist sense, but at the promptings of the divine within. This he felt helped to give purpose and direction to his life.

Several years ago, however, he stopped attending Meeting for Worship, as it "was not connecting with me spiritually at all", though he still feels a "spiritual connection with Quaker ideology/ principles". He has kept links with the Meeting and Friends in it through the writing and cycling groups. For a while he also came to midweek meeting discussions sometimes, and contributed on several occasions to Travellers' Tales sessions after our shared lunches. He is not involved in any other faith group, and his current spiritual experiences come through "cultural and literary 'vehicles'" and through Nature, which "still holds a great place in my life". His most recent comments confirm that he does not feel the need to be part of a group, and is not actively searching for a new spiritual path; but he adds that he is still aware of "a degree of unfulfilled potential in my spiritual life", that his "spiritual place" could be seen as "under review" or "work in progress."

In his original interview, **Dave's** experience of Friends was a largely positive one, the only exception being a course he began studying at his Meeting which was "overly Bible-based, overly Jesus Christ-focused". It was moving in the evangelical direction which he had been trying to escape, and which didn't seem in keeping with what he saw as the Universalist perspectives of most Friends. But on the whole he felt he "gets a lot from" Meeting for Worship and belonging to his Meeting, and was grateful for Friends' unobtrusive support for him in his illness (ME). He was inspired by the lives and writings of Friends over the centuries, and felt Friends in general provide support and examples to follow, though he was conscious of how far he fell short: "Friends provide the collective and individual perspective that has meaning for me", "I'm not looking for any further framework or system." This Quaker background had helped him to live out his faith in his professional work with disability issues, and his voluntary work with Amnesty International. He was sure he had found his spiritual home among Friends: "After over thirty years of looking I've finally found where I need to be"; "I don't envisage that I'll be going anywhere else."

Much of this still remained true for him when I contacted him again a few years later: "I think I'll always remain a Quaker, as the content of the Meeting and the language used 'speak' to me." But, even before moving house in November 2007, he had stopped attending his Local Meeting, which was too small (with attendances sometimes as low as between two and four) to provide much spiritual nurture, and has since closed. As mentioned in the last chapter, he and his wife began attending a local Methodist chapel quite near their new home, soon after moving, and for a time felt they had found "something of a spiritual home" there.

More recently, though, things have changed again, and, while his wife still continues to worship at the chapel, Dave has become an active member of his Local Meeting, and has been on a Quaker Voluntary Action working retreat in Palestine/Israel, which has inspired him to become "involved with other Friends in trying to establish a positive dialogue with Jewish and Muslim communities" in a nearby city.

Kevin and Michelle both have a long and very mixed experience of Friends. **Michelle's** turbulent family life had made her relish the silence: "the peace and serenity were very welcome". She found in Friends an "alternative family" in her early years with them. They were "very thoughtful and calm and I was treated with a lot of respect". This was "so important" to her at a difficult time and she became a member at the age of sixteen, then continued to attend Meeting while away at university, though less so during her social work training. After qualifying she moved to our area and attended her previous Meeting for many years. During this time, she has felt sometimes less, sometimes more, connected to Friends. In her original interview she valued the freedom to explore feelings of oneness and connectedness without barriers of language or having to worry about "what I'm supposed to believe, what the right answers are." And Friends have sparked off in her interest in such areas as non-violence and pacifism. Feminism seemed to fit in well at first, since Quakers lack the patriarchal structure of many churches, but she felt that they still retain some elements of patriarchy and hierarchy, sometimes also getting "caught up in busyness", losing the "core business" of the spiritual basis of their work and making the work itself the core. Friends, she felt, don't "take kindly to passion, abandonment, excess": if they do "live adventurously", it's in "incredibly worthy ways". There aren't many "madcap Friends". She also felt the process of change within herself at that time because she was going through the menopause, and was "not absolutely sure of what my spirituality needs to be at this point in my life", thinking she might come back to Friends "with renewed commitment", or "go off and do something completely different." But she found help in the small groups connected with our Meeting, such as the writing group and Hearts and Minds Prepared, where there was "quite deep sharing" which "held me" at this time of change.

Writing in 2008, Michelle felt still more strongly that physical changes brought about by the menopause "have been echoed in my spiritual journey" and have made her "long-standing unease with patriarchal religious traditions…a more strident discomfort." Quakerism, in her view, continues these "albeit in a more muted form."

And, having previously felt that "on balance, religious belief is a force for good in the world", she now sympathised more and more "with the view that organised religion in general is a major source of conflict in the world and an obstacle to progress". Even Quakerism is to a degree complicit in this by trying to "square the circle" of being both inside and outside the Christian mainstream.

She wondered if she will no longer be able to "achieve a satisfactory accommodation with Quakerism", yet she missed the "sense of belonging to a spiritual community", particularly the kind of spiritual community Friends can provide. Having left full-time employment, "and so facing another major change in my life", she felt she is in "something of a spiritual retreat, though open to new leadings of the spirit." Recently she has spoken again of her need for retreat, silence and solitude as a natural reaction to her busy and, in its last years, stressed working life, a response to the menopause, and/or a return to the solitude she had experienced and grown attached to in childhood. Part of her also fears a return to Friends would mean she would have thrust upon her the tasks and duties, and the insistence on "right ordering" which have overburdened her in the past. She is, though, grateful for Friends' "open door" policy, which means she can return if and when the time is right.

Kevin was "quite taken with" Quakerism after his first introduction to it, and found "awesome" the way ministry "resonated" sometimes with what was going on in his life. For instance he was thinking of his cousin's child, who was born with severe autism, when there was ministry about a broken flower in a vase and the beauty of imperfection. He felt that people were "tuning in" in the silence: "It may have been a coincidence, but it happened more than once." "For quite a long time" he was happy with things as they were, including remaining an attender. He felt that if he became a member, pressure would come from Friends and from within himself to take on jobs for the Meeting, as well as to attend Meeting every week rather than "if moved to". Membership would have something of "Catholic duty" about it. But then came the "spiritual high" of his and Michelle's wedding at their local Meeting House. "It was very, very simple" yet "rich": Both he and Michelle felt "spiritually there", surrounded by Ffriends, and everyone there felt "very spiritually connected." Soon afterwards he decided to apply for membership. He had been "so moved by the whole experience", and felt it had been "so much of a gift" to be married in the Quaker manner "with that very special ministry." All this made him want to take things "that step further". The mood of the visit to discuss his membership was also "very warm and inviting and welcoming", and for a time all went well.

Disillusionment set in when he and Michelle moved into a cottage next to the Meeting House as temporary wardens, and felt that neither they nor the workmen making alterations to the cottage were treated properly, and they moved more quickly than they had intended, feeling "some ambivalence" about Quakerism. Then, however, came the "healing" experience (described elsewhere) of buying a house which seemed right for them, and which was owned by Quakers. And though he found it difficult, and/or did not feel the need, to go to Meeting for Worship much, Kevin liked "the freedom and genuine inclusiveness" of being able to come and go as he pleased. He also valued "the more active, interactive" approach of the writing and Hearts and Minds groups rather than "the more passive experience" of "soaking up the silence" in his previous Meeting. For him, it feels good to be able to "give something back", and he felt "more spiritually connected", finding "amazing" the "variety of experiences that people share, and the intimacy of the experience." He and Michelle both eventually felt it right to transfer their membership to our Area Meeting despite some "ambivalence". This was partly a reluctance to be "a member of anything", but on the other hand they didn't wish to "sit on the fence and take the benefits", when they were getting a lot out of the Meeting, and different things from their previous Meeting. He will nevertheless always be grateful for much that that first Meeting and its members have given him.

Now, however, a few years later, he, like Michelle, feels the need at this time in his life for withdrawal from the outside world into the quiet of home and Michelle's companionship. In his case this was initially a reaction to the continuing pressures of working life, but it is continuing after his recent retirement. He values the potential of the Quaker business method and wishes it could be used more in other, perhaps business, contexts, but like Michelle he feels it has become too inward-looking and narrowly focused.

At the time of her original interview, **Sue** rarely felt able to attend Meeting for Worship, needing to spend time on Sundays with her non-Quaker husband and son, but both Quaker worship and the relationship with local Friends were very important to her. She valued the silence and stillness of Meeting for Worship: though she is "a conversational person": "It's been quite important to me to be quiet". There is "a huge quantity of difference in silence in terms of my spiritual response": the silence "establishes the sense of being in place". It felt important to her that her son should take part in children's meeting, and the only thing which "rocked the boat" for her was the Meeting's lack of interest in this in recent years.

A few years after that initial interview, and after about twenty years as an attender, Sue decided to apply for membership. As the interview made clear, she has known for a long time that Quaker worship and the Quaker way of life resonate strongly with her; and for many years she has described herself as a Quaker. But she moved closer to the wish to become a member when, after a period of being overwhelmed by work and family commitments, she was able to have time away from work and could focus for a while on herself and what her own priorities are. A Quaker colleague's reminder of *Advices and Queries* 28 kept coming back to her: "Attend to what love requires of you, which may not be great busyness." She was able to come to Meeting one Sunday around this time, and during deep and moving worship spoke of "what love requires of [us]". As the Meeting ended, her decision to apply for membership had crystallised. However, as she commented to me later, she is not starry-eyed about it: she is well aware that Friends are not always "Quakerly", and that some aspects of Quaker life, such as business meetings, are not for her, at least at present (though since these comments she has had to become more involved in this side of the Meeting, as part of a – hopefully temporary – clerking team). She knows, too, that she can be actively involved in the Meeting in a number of other ways; and the hurt over Friends' attitude to the children's meeting has been softened somewhat because her son was then developing Quaker connections of his own, for instance at Holiday School. She added that she is also even more appreciative of Quaker openness, having encountered a conspicuous lack of it at a recent meeting with Anglicans.

Janet, as we saw earlier, discovered Quakerism through attending Quaker boarding-school: although it fitted in with some of her parents' values, it was "a complete change of world" in its beauty, and in its tolerance, which she saw carried out in practice in its "broad-based" evening readings. We have seen that her time there developed her need for quiet, and for her own space. That "Quaker quiet" has continued to be important to her. Yet in her period of despair she didn't feel Quakerism would help: she "needed a teacher." Nevertheless, the way the Gurdjieff teachers spoke reminded her, as mentioned, of ministry in Meeting for Worship. She went back to Friends many years later when she gave up her work with Gurdjieff groups, and was pleased for her young son to join in the children's activities. She felt that Friends might not be one hundred percent, but at least they knew it, unlike most other people. Again, however, as mentioned earlier, she felt the need for more "guidance" and "structure", and became involved with Buddhism. But later on she again returned to Friends. Times of quiet and reflection are very much part of her spiritual practice, and she feels that she sometimes needs "more contact" with people who "value the spiritual side of life", and at the time of the interview was finding this more among Friends. She very much valued the worship-sharing, which was an important part of Hearts and Minds, and hoped there would in future be more "listening" in our midweek discussion meetings. This is how she sums up the significance of Meeting for Worship for her: "the Quaker quiet hour really helps me to come back into myself – it's like a really good meal for the week." She also values *Advices and Queries* as a way of "constantly checking yourself." Although she has moved away from Meeting again in recent years, she feels her attitudes to it remain essentially the same.

For reflection and sharing

- **How did you discover Quakers?**
- **What were your first impressions?**
- **What do you value about being a Quaker?**
- **What are you less happy with?**

Chapter four

The Inner Journey

The inner spiritual life

Searching and longing. All the respondents have a solitary spiritual life of some kind, an inner awareness of, or need for, a spiritual dimension which has always been there and/or has become stronger in their later years. We have seen that for Wendy, Michelle and Sue, the need and response were there from childhood and satisfied in varying degrees by church (and, for Michelle, Quaker Meeting) attendance, remaining with them. For Sue, the spiritual dimension "never goes away"; "I've never been able to let it drop", even when it has been difficult to stay with it. From childhood, and more markedly in adolescence, Dave felt the stirrings of "a real interest in "Where do we come from?" which has "rumbled along, sometimes in the foreground, sometimes in the background" for many years. In a number of cases, this search has been felt as a lack or an emptiness. We have noted Janet's feeling in her late teens that there was no answer to her questions, no one to help her to understand the madness of the world around her and in herself. Jan has moved away from religion at times, but the need keeps returning: she feels spiritual hunger, even "a kind of grief" without some spiritual outlet. Both Graham and Gwynneth have had long periods when they were too busy with work and family commitments (what Gwynneth described as "work and bed") even to notice any spiritual need, but it has reasserted itself in their later years. This happened to Gwynneth when her second husband died; while Graham in his late forties "experienced a period of spiritual aridity": things had become "so empty on the spiritual front, I needed nurturing in that facet of my life."

This spiritual need has expressed itself partly in the search for a spiritual home, a number of the group searching for many years before finding the place, or places, which seemed to answer their own particular need, as we have seen. But for most, their search has also been, and remains, an individual one, to a large extent because they value the freedom to explore spiritually and resist any attempts to lead them along a particular spiritual path: Gwynneth, you may remember, was not happy with all the "You must's" she encountered in different faith groups: "We're free spirits really, aren't we?" Paul, in his schooldays, "quickly developed a dislike and distrust for organised worship", and is glad that his parents left him free to choose: "That freedom and choice have become the foundations of my spiritual life." For Dave, faith is not something "out there": "It's got to come from the heart… from within"; "We've all got the potential if only we'll allow it to show itself"; "We're all capable of the faith-driven aspect of ourselves" and of taking "individual responsibility" for it. While Janet and David found in Buddhism the teaching, the order and structure which Quakerism might sometimes lack, both valued the freedom Quakerism and their local Meeting have given them.

Sources of spiritual nourishment

Nature. A number of respondents have found their most intense spiritual experiences through the natural world, experiences which they usually first encountered early in life, but which have remained important to them ever since. We have seen that Gwynneth and Paul had their first such experiences in childhood, while Graham and Dave became aware of them as teenagers. "It was at times like that" [long solitary walks in the country] "that I did have a sense of something infinitely greater, more powerful, but it wasn't the God I'd previously identified with, but there was something there and that was important to me."(Graham). Cycling in the local countryside from his early teens, Dave had "moments of intense awareness of self" and of "the world around me", which aroused in him a sense of wonder. He wasn't sure if this was "specifically religious", though it did give him the feeling that "there must be some force of some kind that created all this". Michelle rejoices in the "wastefulness", the "extravagance" in Nature – the over-abundance of a particular colour for example – and sees God as a "passionate artist." Jan responds with awe to the natural world and has a fascination with the sea, also feeling that so much beauty betokens a higher intelligence. Kevin loves the spiritual quality of the early morning, discovered when doing a paper round as a boy, then when working as a postman for a time: "I do like the world when it's new…when it's unsullied and nobody's messed it up yet." For Wendy, her experience of Nature is more of a background to her religious faith, but in recent years she has become "fascinated" by the miracle of spring, and has always felt a deep response to the hills, which are both "awesome" and "comforting."

As an extension of this, Graham has also mentioned the importance of travel, at least in some of the counties he has visited, for instance during a visit to South Africa: "The nature of the relationship between the country and its values, hopes, ambitions and shames… was something South Africa registered with me very deeply – and gave me, I would say, a spiritual experience…"

The arts. We have seen the aesthetic appeal of formal worship even in childhood for some respondents, and the way Sue encountered this particularly strongly at the High Anglican church she attended during her student days, "linking religious thought with aesthetics." Jan goes on feeling "the power within music" she sensed in hymns as a child, and singing in a choir and listening to music are important to her, as she found anew in France. Sue feels that the "silent listening, still state of mind" of Meeting for Worship "is the same right-brained state in which creative acts are undertaken", the same energy, and she sees "artistic endeavour " as "an attempt at truth, an aspiration towards authenticity about the human condition and the heights and depths of what human beings are capable of."

Several respondents are themselves involved in "artistic endeavour", seeking, for instance, to express their spiritual experiences in prose or poetry; and/or find a spiritual dimension in others' works of art to which they respond strongly. Graham, for one, feels intensely the "power and beauty" of opera, and of writing, particularly in certain novels and poems, seeing both words and music engaged in the deep exploration of "powerful human emotions and experiences."

Spirituality and everyday life. But Sue among others emphasised that spiritual experience is also simply part of our everyday lives. People, she said, write about spiritual experience as if it's "other" and "alien", but it happens all the time, not "great big flashing, blinding light", but "a lot of low-grade stuff". It can be anywhere, any time – "it's within" – so we don't need to try deliberately to access it or give it a slot on the calendar, for there's "spiritual grace all over the place." She might think of the names of people she's concerned about as she cycles along – a way of praying – and "when in a stew about something" she has found a calm through digging the garden – a "physical, repeated activity" – that she hadn't felt in Meeting for Worship. For Dave, an intense awareness of the present moment, in whatever circumstances, has a spiritual dimension which he sometimes seeks to express in his writing: "an intensity of the time and of the moment, which gives an added depth to understanding who I am in the larger scale of things", a sense that "we're all part of something infinitely larger that we can only occasionally glimpse the significance of." Michelle feels that there are "many things that aren't very worthy which speak to me of God": – laughter, sex, luxury, also "passion, abandonment, excess" – qualities which, as we've seen, she finds in Nature too, in God's creativity.

Several made the point that spirituality or any religious faith has to relate to the real world and provide a basis for ethical living: While Graham felt his spiritual experiences through nature are "separate and special", he nonetheless thought that the promptings of the divine within and "answering that of God in everyone" helped him to treat others with respect, to do what he can to make life better and more enriching. Wendy felt it was important to live out your faith: as one of her uncles said, it's no good being "a Sunday saint and a Monday devil". Jan was not happy with the Christadelphians' pulling away from the world: she prefers life as it is and wants to live as good a life as possible. David stressed the importance of being not only "spiritually whole" but being useful as well, when he said: "I'm not a believer in Cloud Nine!"

Illness has taught Dave the importance of being as well as doing, but for him, as for others, work has been of crucial significance in living out his own faith. Though he had to take early retirement on health grounds, he continued to be involved to some extent in disability issues in education: "It's who I am", "it's what I get personal as well as professional satisfaction from". He has also tried to live out his faith through his voluntary work for Amnesty Inernational. Both Kevin and Michelle also saw their probation work as spiritually based. Michelle found her work helped her to feel closer to God, giving her a sense of "God in the room" alongside herself and her client. For Kevin, visiting a young boy in Borstal during his student days was "a very important moment" in his career choice, though he didn't realise it at the time. He could see "how alone this lad was, and how messed up in many areas." It gave him a sense of "There but for the grace of God go I". While there was nothing explicitly spiritual about his later decision to go into the probation service, "that unarticulated sense of 'that of God' or good in everyone was very much why I wanted to do it", and he has always tried to discern that "saving grace" and separate what were often "horrific" acts from the person who carried them out, though this has sometimes been very difficult.

Leadings. Kevin's initial "important moment" in his career choice was, he realised later, a moment when he felt the Spirit pulling in a particular direction, which was further confirmed when he met a few people in the probation service at a drama group he attended. Much later in his life he felt there was "some sort of guiding hand" in the way he and Michelle came upon their present house, discovering the owners were Quakers and finding the purchase went through very smoothly, and that there were "good vibes" in the house, a sense of "peace and tranquillity" coming not only from the Quaker owners but from other previous inhabitants of the house. It was all "quite healing, most unlooked-for", especially after bruising experiences with their previous Meeting. For Michelle, the Spirit can also pull in completely unexpected directions and show us we are not in control of our lives: Kevin had just had a vasectomy when they found they had to take over the care of the daughter of a close friend. For many, the unexpectedness and suddenness of spiritual experiences, particularly in Nature, seemed to open new doors for them. As we have seen, other leadings were closely connected with the respondents' discovery of Quakerism.

Influences and affinities. Some of these, which were also connected with Quaker experience, have already been mentioned, but there were other important influences and affinities on their spiritual journeys for most respondents, mainly through people they had known well, encountered briefly, or known indirectly through their writings and broadcasts, though occasionally places, too, played an important role. Graham felt there was no one significant influence, but that many people had played a part in his spiritual development, through things they had said or passages he had read in their books.

Early influences naturally included parents and teachers. Wendy was particularly influenced by her father, a Methodist lay preacher, and also by one of her Sunday school teachers. Both combined strong faith with living out their religion. Gwynneth, particularly, remembers her maternal grandmother and her father, both strict but loving, and both with strong beliefs, though neither preached at their children and grandchildren. For Jan, too, her maternal grandmother was an important figure: she was a Congregationalist but thought highly of Friends, and like them disliked outward show, for instance dressing very simply at her second wedding in her later years. She felt close, too, to an old lady who took her under her wing when she joined the church choir as a child. For Kevin, his mother's strong Roman Catholic faith was important, as was her acceptance of her children's decisions to leave the Church. He greatly admired, too, his Latin teacher, who cared about every one of his pupils, and who died quite young, with "virtually the entire school" attending his funeral; also the third of three priests he had known in boyhood who quietly persisted in his vocation long after his two colleagues had given theirs up.

Later on, partners were often a strong spiritual influence, whether or not they belonged to a faith group. Wendy and Kevin admire their partner's strong commitment to Quakerism and the way each lives it out. Sue's husband rejects organised religion, but has his own combination of mysticism and physics. Gwynneth's late second husband was not formally religious, but she feels he was an "enlightened soul", who would approve of her spiritual search now, while Jan feels that her second husband, who has no formal religious ties either, is strongly spiritual in his love of Nature and deep environmental concerns. Several respondents mentioned being impressed by colleagues or friends with a strong religious faith: Dave, for instance, had worked with a woman who was "a staunch Methodist". "It wasn't what she said, but what she did": she was "a person who tried to live her beliefs", open about her religious views but not thrusting them down people's throats. We have seen, too, that he has been impressed by the goodness of individuals and faith groups, whether or not he shares their beliefs, for instance the mutual toleration of Muslims and Christians in Ethiopia, or the Salvation Army, who are "on the front line" when it comes to caring for others, and who showed "real concern" for his mother, who attended one of their churches, when she was ill. For Sue, there is also a sense that there is something in common between herself and people of any faith "who are interested in their spiritual life": there are differences of belief and practice, but also "a common element, which we seem to recognise in one another" (one of her closest friends is a Hindu, and she has found this with Jewish people too).

For others, the key influences were those of a teacher or guide, who often seemed to appear at the right stage in their lives. Janet is thankful for the wise and understanding teachers who have deepened her knowledge of Gurdjieff's teachings over the years. For Gwynneth, her mentors were the equally wise and understanding teachers who opened doors to religion and philosophy for her in her later years, particularly the Hindu teacher whose wise sayings she treasures. David, particularly, remembered certain Buddhist teachers, among them the Dalai Lama himself, but also the lay teacher who later became ordained, "so clear, very penetrating and challenging" and the Tibetan monk whose classes he attended in London.

Often closely allied with this "live" teaching are the written and broadcast words of teachers, as in several respondents' discovery of Quakerism. David found that certain parts of Christian Science's *Science and Health* are "very thought-provoking and interesting, and have a lot of spiritual insight." We have already seen the particular impact on him of a Tibetan monk's *The Tibetan Book of Living and Dying*, and he also mentioned an eleventh-century Buddhist text on "how to conduct the spiritual life, the snags on the way and how to deal with them." Similarly, Janet values cassettes of the Buddhist monk Thich Nhat Hanh and incorporates sections of them into her daily spiritual practice. For Dave, a wide variety of books, radio and TV programmes have been important, perhaps especially when he has not been involved with any faith group. He particularly mentioned books by Karen Armstrong, like *A History of God*; the TV series "Two Thousand Years of Christianity" and "The Sea of Faith", plus the book of the same name, as well as speakers on the "Thought for the Day" slot on Radio 4's Today programme, such as Richard Harries, then Bishop of Oxford, or Rabbi Lionel Blue, who have "a degree of wisdom that cuts across any faith perspective." He also values the Old Testament/Hebrew Bible and wishes there was more awareness of it.

We have seen that places have also played an important part for some: particular stretches of countryside, or places of worship. For Gwynneth, the Findhorn Foundation has been a very special place, with its sense of community and connection with Nature, and its way of leading her into meditation and "inner listening". Michelle is fascinated by the temples to female deities on the island of Gozo, to which she often returns: they are part of her search for female voices in the different religions.

Spiritual practice and prayer. All respondents have some kind of individual spiritual practice outside Meeting for Worship, though this is often fairly unstructured and informal, like becoming aware of a divine presence through Nature when walking or cycling, or reading books on spiritual themes. Few made explicit reference to prayer, though, as already noted, Sue spoke of thinking of the names of people she was concerned about while cycling. She had also experienced the strong support of others' prayers when her mother was in a coma some years ago. She and other members of her family had "no energy" to pray themselves, yet "people did it for us", "you could touch it almost", it was like "a great protective blanket around all of us" and "one of the most powerful things that [has] happened to me." Prayer is a very important part of Wendy's life, "in my everyday life and in my church life". Apart from having a few minutes' prayer time first thing in the morning or last thing at night, there is "no set place or set time or set routine" as "God is with you all the time": it happens "when I'm doing ordinary things" like ironing or drying up. She believes strongly in "the power of prayer" and that it can "bring answers – not always what you want." She prays for members of her family in difficult situations and is sure "it's prayer that brought them through."

Other respondents have a regular or even daily spiritual practice, though not based in prayer in the conventional sense. Jan feels the need for "just sitting there quietly", though readings from the Bible or other spiritual books "feed" her. At such times – though it can also be in ordinary conversation – she has a sense of "power" speaking directly to her, bringing a "dawning realisation." Of all the respondents, Janet has perhaps the most developed spiritual practice, which she has worked out for herself from several different traditions. She has a daily morning practice, when she sits for at least ten minutes cross-legged on a cushion in a particular place, beginning with the Gurdjieff practice of "coming into your body", checking the body limb by limb, if necessary adding internal prayers or chanting to calm the "chattering" mind. She then listens to sections of Thich Nhat Hanh's cassettes, which give a very good explanation of "how to put Buddhism into practice" and these provide food for thought for the day. She also has a practice at the end of the day, where she sits up in bed or on the cushion and thinks about how the day has gone, often saying the Lord's Prayer or the twenty-third Psalm, "for closure on the day" or the Buddhist "go for refuge" prayer. She will also try to "come back into that place" from time to time during the day, for instance when walking – "being present to what you're doing." She likes to have even a short time at regular intervals for the spiritual dimension of her life, "so that it permeates my ordinary life as well". If things are too stimulating, "too demanding" or "too stressful out in the world", she loses touch "with that other part of myself". It is easy to forget it when she needs it most, and it is important to try to "remember that it can be there…available all the time", important to have that routine so that she doesn't get "entirely wrapped up in the world-game".

"What's it all about?" – beliefs, values and meanings

Ideas of God/Spirit. Wendy's idea of God has become stronger as she has got older, though she feels it perhaps remains "childish" in some ways: someone watching over us, who is "with you all the time" and is "loving and faithful", giving us strength and support in difficult times. She believes strongly in "that of God in everyone." Though Sue speaks of God in Trinitarian language, and would accept the word "Father" which appeals to her more than "Son" or "Holy Spirit" (the latter overused in evangelical circles, she feels), it is because "'Father' is the "generative, creative part of the Trinity." In the past, she has had difficulties with the word "God" because of the "lack of intellectual rigour" of the Anglican approach, but she is less concerned about this now, more aware of other levels of experience, of "the regenerative qualities of the unconscious mind" emphasised in current psychological thinking.

Both Graham and Dave emphasise God's role as Creator. In contemplating the vastness of the universe, Graham has a sense of some other "very powerful and all-knowing force" at work; Dave, too, from his teenage years had the feeling that "there must be some force of some kind that created all this". Both also, however, have a sense of the divine within: Graham speaks of the divine promptings within leading us to try to make life better for others; Dave of faith coming "from the heart", "from within". While Graham would use the word "God", Dave prefers "faith" or "spirit". Seeing God in personal terms, he feels, "diminishes" the divine; and seeing God as male is a reflection of past attitudes: "it limits [God] within the human frame", as does the notion of "a quick prayer to God": for him, this "belittles faith." For Michelle, too, there is a strong sense of God as Creator, "a passionate artist", and as a force both within and outside ourselves, both as "internal and individual", and as "other", "external reality", almost as "divine supervisor" in her work. She has also moved very far away from the notion of a "male" God: she is very interested in female deities, and feels that they are "much more rooted in the earth and in blood", in the body and reproduction, a connection that has been lost in the mainstream, patriarchal religions. She feels that now she is looking for the female aspects of different religions, rather than for one particular religion.

David saw God as neither personal nor transcendent, emphasising instead the "immanent God, who dwells in the human heart", guiding us spiritually and ethically. He found valuable the Christian Science "very lofty concept of God", which is not a personal one, and for him its founder Mrs Eddy's seven synonyms for God – "Mind", "Soul", "Spirit", "Principle", "Life", "Truth", "Love" – were a "rich source for contemplation." He personally liked "Principle", with its idea of a "lawgiver", an orderly universe. Others, too, have different "synonyms" for God. Gwynneth, for instance, now speaks of the "Universal Energy", and she "tunes into it" through "inner listening", the process she discovered at Findhorn. Though she says that "for years I didn't like the word 'God', she now feels people can say what they like. Janet too would now accept the word, but not the anthropomorphic idea of God, which lands people in a mess when they try to reconcile a "caring God" with natural disasters. Gurdjieff used the term, "Absolute"; she herself would speak of "pattern", "balance", "organisation." She feels, too, that there is "a knowing in all of us" which can provide guidance, and some would call this God; but, to access it, we need to be in a quieter, calmer place physically and/or mentally. Paul does not specifically use the word "God", but talks of "connection": "a connection so deep and satisfying" in the "October orchard", and, more specifically, how attendance at Meeting for Worship was developing "a gentle connection with that Divine reality which I believe is present behind everything." Kevin, like Gwynneth, tends to see God in terms of energy, and, above all, as mysterious and unknowable. "That of God", an important phrase for him, is difficult to pin down, but he sees it as "some sort of essence" within people, and plants and animals too. He feels that images of God are all the more powerful for him for being vaguer: "It's about that essence really, that life-force, that strange mystery."

Jesus and Christianity. For Graham, among others, the childhood "comforting" literal belief in an "all-caring" Jesus has long since vanished. Though in some ways the most orthodox Christian in the group, generally accepting teachings about Jesus, Wendy tends to put her main emphasis on her relationship with God, while Jan, drawn more to the "Christ-figure" when young, now feels God is "the real boss." Several respondents saw stories about Jesus as symbolic, a "recurring myth" (Kevin); an "important narrative" and "myth" (Michelle), stories that are to be taken symbolically and metaphorically, that "resonate with something deep within us" (Sue). Jan felt the crucifixion and resurrection stories are "metaphors" for something deeper. For Kevin, these symbolic interpretations emphasise the mystery of Jesus and are "all the more powerful" for not being located in a particular time, nor linked with the "gruesome fascination" with the crucified Christ, with which he had been brought up.

Jesus was seen by several, too, as an ethical example and teacher above all, with little importance attached to the truth, or otherwise, of accounts of his life: a "model for human behaviour" (Michelle); "symbolic of Christian values and the Christian faith rather than me having a literal belief in all that has been written about him and his life"(Graham); his "message" is the "basis of Quaker faith" and more important than whether he existed (Dave). Graham did feel, though, that he and perhaps many others needed "the attachment to a recognisable 'individual' "to make "much of what the Christian faith is about…accessible [and] believable." And Sue would want to reclaim the name "Christian" from the evangelicals (though knows other Christians wouldn't consider her one!): "The Christian tradition has given me a language and stories which help me to talk about parts of my experience" that she couldn't express otherwise; she keeps getting drawn back to the stories, trying to work out "what's going on", "what it really means". For her, it's all "such an enigma": "there's nothing clear about Jesus." Despite her "dissatisfactions, institutional and philosophical" with Christianity, she still feels part of it, and has no personal leaning towards other faiths, despite her sense of affinity with deeply spiritual people of any faith.

Evil, suffering, death – and an afterlife? As we have seen, to some extent, in their accounts of their outer journeys, most respondents had known deep suffering at some time in their lives: Janet, for instance, the death of her father when she was only eleven, Gwynneth the death of her beloved second husband after which she became a "hermit" for some time, Jan the premature death of her brother and, though she was too young to remember it consciously, she has been profoundly affected by the accidental death of her sister, who was only four at the time. David's wife and mother both died of cancer, perhaps unnecessarily, "under Christian Science treatment"; Dave has suffered from ME for a number of years, Graham from depression. Several had suffered at the hands of other people too, most notably Gwynneth and Jan, whose first husbands deserted them for another partner. Some also felt for others' pain and suffering: Wendy for instance felt that she herself is "an absolute wimp" about pain and suffering, but also "can't bear to see anyone in pain", physical or otherwise: she "can't help but suffer with them", whether they are near neighbours or far away, as at the time of the tsunami on Boxing Day 2004.

Most seem, however, to have been resilient and able to move on and make a good life for themselves: Gwynneth and Jan going on, for instance, to make happy second marriages, and Gwynneth in her later years entering a period of spiritual exploration. There is little or no railing against God or Fate, and no sense of evil as an external force. For several (Graham, Dave, Wendy and Janet), the 2004 tsunami (which was much in people's minds, as most of these interviews were conducted a few months later) was simply a natural event: Janet felt attributing it to God was a product of the confusion caused by the superhuman, anthropomorphic notion of God as a person who protects us or punishes us. Dave saw its positive – but not supernatural – effects: it was a "wake-up call" not to take things for granted, and a "challenge", giving us a choice to make a positive response. He also feels that his illness has taught him important things, to take things less for granted, to be appreciative of each day, to "be" rather than "do", and it has brought himself and his wife closer together. There was a sense among the respondents, too, that rather than being an "act of God", much of the suffering in the world is caused by human beings – "that sort of pain doesn't need to be", said Wendy – or indeed by oneself, by one's own attitude to events, in David's Buddhist interpretation. Sue's sense of human beings' part in all this is more complex. "We all have huge potential within us for good and for evil." For both Wendy and David, death, pain and suffering are part of life and have to be accepted as inevitable, essentially unchangeable, but, as David added, that doesn't necessarily mean we just "lie down and die". "People can fight back in the most amazing ways." And God was not necessarily seen as detached from our suffering: Wendy, indeed, felt that God "puts [suffering] there for a purpose" at times, "for our own good", but also that he "gives us the strength to cope" with difficulties in our lives. Sue didn't see God as "the creator of suffering", but as "what's left" – "the creative response in suffering [itself]".

Dying was rarely mentioned in reflections on death and its aftermath. Wendy, however, stressed the importance of dying with dignity, rather than lingering on in great pain or after the loss of our faculties, while accepting that this is rarely something that can be arranged. She has some fear of death itself (her father once said he wouldn't fear death, and she wishes she had asked him why), partly because of the possibility of being either buried or cremated alive. But she does have a sense that there is "something beyond", and hopes, but isn't certain, that she will meet loved ones again there. She thinks there is "somewhere you might go" if you have been really wicked, though even then has a feeling that if you "repent at the last hurdle", all but the worst sinners "will enter the kingdom of God." Sue does believe in the immortality of the soul, though "struggles" with the resurrection of the body.

Others had even less definite views on what might happen after death. Jan spoke for several in emphasising the essential mystery of this, mentioning her younger daughter's thoughts about the energy released when people die – "Where does all that energy go?" – and her elder daughter's claim that people have been seen after their death, though Jan herself has doubts about spiritualism. She does, however, have a sense that her mother is still with her and, an exile from her native country during her lifetime, has been able in some way to return through Jan, who came to live there. Kevin saw two possibilities in the central mystery, and oscillated between them, "continu[ing] evolving on some other plane", though this could be rather depressing, going on "not getting it"; or "energy returning to a central locus", which "doesn't depress or scare me really". There were similar ideas from Michelle, who saw death as a recycling of energy, and Janet, who felt her own molecules would continue in some form: she has an open mind on reincarnation. Of all the respondents, Graham was the one who most explicitly rejected any notion of an afterlife. Indeed, he had a sense of "individual dispensability": "Anyone who fears death has an inflated notion of their own significance – we're all very temporary", which was to some extent shared by Michelle, who felt the whole notion of resurrection seems selfish, tantamount to saying, "I will retain my identity".

For a number of respondents, life here and now is precious, and they were content to accept that what happens afterwards remains a mystery. David stressed the importance of the Buddhist awareness of death, and commented that the concept of reincarnation is difficult for Westerners to understand, but did not speculate further on what happens after death, being firmly anchored to this life. Similarly, Janet pointed out that she won't know anyway whether she has been reincarnated or not. And Dave felt he has things to say and do before he dies.

When it came to having their lives remembered and celebrated, Graham and Michelle had no interest in this. Michelle preferred the Buddhist idea of non-attachment: "you engage with the world but you haven't got self/ego invested in it." Graham, indeed, did not have even an active desire to continue living and achieve more: he felt he has done all he is going to do, though acknowledged that all this may be influenced by his periods of depression. And those who did suggest how they might wish to be remembered focused on how they have tried to behave in this life: Dave would like to be remembered for helping people, Wendy for "liv[ing] my Christian life", not just being a "Sunday Christian." Or they suggested ceremonies which would emphasise how much they had valued life and what joy it had brought them: Sue wanted to "go out with a bit of oomph", and stressed the importance of celebration, though not in a "triumphalist" way. And David, too, wanted his life to be celebrated in the Meeting House with all the lights on, and no one wearing black. His memorial Meeting for Worship was, indeed, a joyous as well as a sad occasion, as many of his Ffriends, colleagues and students told of the warmth, encouragement, support and sheer fun he had brought into their lives, and gave heartfelt thanks for his.

For reflection and sharing

- **What kind of experiences would you describe as "spiritual" in your life?**
- **What are your beliefs about God/Spirit, Jesus and Christianity (or another faith), evil, suffering, death and its aftermath?**
- **Who or what is most important to you/gives your life meaning and purpose?**

Chapter five

New Ways of Believing and Belonging

Varieties of spiritual exploration

Are our spiritual explorers an unusual, even unique, group in today's world? How do they fit into the wider picture?

The conventional wisdom seems to be that, in Europe at least, society is becoming more and more secular. Certainly, church attendances continue to decline; many people have rejected the beliefs they were brought up with, and are now indifferent, or even hostile to, religion; and an increasing number have had no contact with religion and see it as archaic and irrelevant to their lives. In recent years, a new, more militant atheism – as in Richard Dawkins' *The God Delusion* – seems to have emerged.

At the opposite extreme, numbers in evangelical and fundamentalist congregations go on growing, as if some are seeking religious certainty as a refuge from the change, doubt and questioning around them. For we live in a time of searching and questioning about the meaning of life and the place of religion in our lives, and in between the two extremes, we find many forms of spiritual exploration. Contemporary writers – who perhaps both influence and respond to the shifting situation around them – provide commentaries on two main strands: the changing face of religion and the apparently new emphasis on spirituality.

From the mid-twentieth century onwards there have been new definitions of God and Christianity, not only from John Robinson, but also from Dietrich Bonhoeffer and Paul Tillich, among others, and new views of Jesus from John Hick and others, including liberation theologians. As we approached, then entered, the new millennium, writers like Marcus Borg, John Shelby Spong and Harvey Cox have portrayed a new kind of Christianity, more in tune with our conemporary view of the world.

And, as we came into the twenty-first century, other writers described a new spirituality, which sees itself as distinct from religion, or crosses religious divides. David Tacey defined it as "the perennial search for connectedness to something greater than ourselves, however we wish to name or experience that greater reality", emphasising its ancient and universal quality as well as its contemporary Western form. For Robert Forman, "Grassroots spirituality involves a vaguely panentheistic ultimate that is indwelling…in the deepest self…" His "ultimate" seems to be another name for Tacey's "greater reality"; "panentheistic" suggests it is present in all creation as well as in "the deepest self", and so seems to be similar to Wordsworth's "spirit that…rolls through all things". Both writers seem optimistic that this "grassroots spirituality", though essentially based in individual, inner experience, connects us to other people and will continue to grow and spread, becoming more influential and helping humanity to unite to combat the many threats and crises that face us.

Both the explorers seeking a new kind of religion and those describing themselves as "spiritual" emphasise their freedom to explore, to plough their own furrow within or outside religion. Yet both sets of writers also seem to advocate a communal approach, working together to reconstruct Christianity, or joining with others to create a worldwide spirituality movement. While some explorers do not feel the need to be part of a community, many others, Quakers and non-Quakers, are also searching for a spiritual home, and to a greater or lesser degree experience inner conflict between the desire to explore freely and the longing to be part of a spiritual community – we have seen something of this with our Quaker explorers.

These conflicting desires reflect trends in society at large. It has become a commonplace to say that human beings, at least in Western societies, are becoming more individualistic, alienated, "non-joiners", less willing – or, for various reasons, less able – to join religious, political or social groups and even lacking any sense of community. Yet, at the same time, there is a growing feeling of isolation for many, a dissatisfaction with their present lifestyle, and people are seeking to build new forms of community. Social networking websites, reading groups, Weight Watchers and Transition Town initiatives are four disparate examples of community-building that spring to mind, but there are many others.

There seems to be a spectrum of spiritual exploration: at one end, the desire for complete freedom to explore dominates; as we approach the other end, it is the search for a spiritual home which grows more important, though always with a measure of spiritual independence.

At the "freedom" end are probably many who could be called "devout sceptics", as they are described by Bel Mooney in her Radio 4 series and her book of the same name. They value deep connections with other people, with Nature or the arts, for example, but do not see these as religious or spiritual experiences, and are completely independent in that they feel no inclination to join a faith group or delve more deeply into these special experiences.

Others are described by Grace Davie as "believing without belonging" (the subtitle of her book, *Religion in Britain since 1945*, 2002) – a phrase I have adapted for the title of this chapter. She notes that a number of people hold some religious beliefs without feeling the need to belong to a faith group.

Like many Quaker explorers, yet others are "jigsaw people", trying out several faith groups in turn, or simultaneously. They may eventually settle on one in particular, but will often "pick and mix" the aspects of each which they find most appealing, or will continue to alternate between different places of worship, retaining their freedom and refusing to be pinned down or "labelled". John, a counsellor and psychotherapist, and one of the non-Quaker spiritual explorers whom I met at our small local retreat house, is fascinated by the many links as well as contrasts between different faiths. He and Mike, a chaplain in a psychiatric hospital, see respecting and nurturing each client's unique spirituality as a vital part of their work.

Some have managed to find fellow-explorers without necessarily needing to make a strong commitment, and while continuing their individual search. One way to do this is to set up, or join, a small informal group which meets regularly, with others who are searching too. The groups can combine silence and sharing, as in the Quaker Experiment with Light, Writing the Spirit and spiritual friendship groups. Or it may be mainly based in silence, for instance in healing or meditation groups, or the ecumenical Julian Meetings for contemplative prayer. Joining others for discussion as well as reflection is also helpful, either within one's own faith group, or in an ecumenical group, like the one which met for a time at a church near us and sought to reflect and explore freely, or the groups attending the courses formerly held at our local retreat house. Others who feel restricted within their own faith group may form their own discussion group outside it, like a group known to me outside our immediate area, which discusses radical Christian writings, like those of Bishop Spong.

There are those who appreciate instead, or as well, the chance to form temporary communities, where they can reflect in solitude or in silent company with others, and/or can explore and express their reflections more freely with strangers than they can with those well known to them. Day and weekend conferences, and particularly retreats and quiet days, or retreats combining work and worship, like Quaker Voluntary Action's working retreats, give such opportunities.

Another way of connecting with others, with still more freedom to explore, is through networks like the Living Spirituality Network (sadly now laid down), the Progressive Christianity Network (PCN), or CANA (Christians Awakening to New Awareness), which, through newsletters and mailing lists, provide book reviews, offer new ideas in articles, and supply information on – or organise themselves – courses, conferences and retreats.

Those who feel most torn between the freedom to explore and remaining part of a faith community, to which they are in some ways deeply attached, are often questioning spirits within a particular faith group, most notably within one or other of the Christian denominations. As part of her talk, "Beyond the Spirituality Revolution" at the Living Spirituality Network's Final Gathering, on April 21st 2012, its Director, Eley McAinsh, described interviews with twenty one people from diverse backgrounds, recorded at, or as a result of, a day on "The 'turn' to spirituality", held at Sarum College, Salisbury, in February 2011. Eley found among most, if not all of them, "a strong sense of independent enquiry and exploration", an attempt to "make sense of their own spiritual experience", which "traditional teaching and doctrine" had failed to help them with. While most have remained with their particular church, though often provisionally and "marginally"; a "significant minority" have felt driven to leave, at least for the time being. All have "a deep longing for community" and a connection with those of like mind, but have discovered "these are the hardest things to find, both in and out of the religious institutions." My own conversations with people following their own path within Christianity, sometimes on its fringes, but sometimes at the heart of it, seem to bear out Eley's conclusions.

In *A Churchless Faith* (2002), Alan Jamieson shows how, in spite of these conflicting desires, communal action can be taken by those feeling marginalised within their church. He describes how some Christians in New Zealand, particularly former members of evangelical churches who have become disenchanted with them, are setting up worshipping groups of their own and developing their own rituals, perhaps finding new ways of exploring spiritually together.

For yet others, the spiritual home appears (at least at first) to be more important than spiritual exploration. Brian Mountford describes what he calls "Christian atheism" (*Christian Atheist*, 2011. Incidentally, the book's subtitle, also adapted from Grace Davie's book, is "belonging without believing"). He sees atheists or humanists who attend church as not only valuing its fellowship and seeing its aesthetic appeal, but sharing the same desire for justice and love as Christian believers. Eventually, he feels, "[both groups] might come to see that each is talking the same language" (pp. 114-15).

Still less obviously religious, but maybe in their own way spiritual, are the "Sunday Assemblies" we are beginning to hear about, in cities in the UK and other English-speaking countries, whose adherents reject religious belief, but sing, reflect on life's big questions and give practical help to others, taking as their motto "to live better, help often and wonder more" (information gleaned from *The Times*, September 16th 2013, and BBC Radio 4, November 2nd 2013 and February 24th 2014).

However, these two groups are not only finding new ways of belonging: as Brian Mountford asserts, they are working out their own ways of expressing their deepest concerns, and may, as he also suggests, be sharing the same experiences as their more orthodox friends, but describing them differently.

Quakers' role in spiritual exploration: some personal reflections
My own experience, and the interviews and other examples contained here, have begun to suggest to me that these contemporary views of spirituality have much in common, as David Tacey asserts, with ancient forms of spiritual experience, particularly mysticism (a directly experienced sense of union with God/Spirit). They also suggest that that popular views – and some dictionary definitions – of mysticism as inward-looking, vague and divorced from reality, or granted only to an elite few, are mistaken, or at least do not tell the whole story.

So I was very interested to hear the thoughts of Eley McAinsh of the Living Spirituality Network, who led a day conference on "Mysticism and Contemporary Spirituality" at St. Mark's Centre for Radical Christianity, Sheffield, in November 2010. She inclined to the view that mystical experience is not just for the few, but is "a transforming gift, available to anyone attentive enough to receive it", and sees it as often closely linked to action, rather than detached from everyday reality. She agreed with the German liberation theologian Dorothee Soelle, who saw it as the experiencing and then acting out of God's love, practically and politically, in the world. Roswitha Jarman, too, emphasises this link between mystical experience and love in action in her Kindlers booklet, *Breakthrough to Unity* (2010).

Eley also saw close connections between mysticism and contemporary spirituality: both are based on direct personal experience of the divine in some form, which may inspire us to action; indeed she felt that it may be that, at this time of crisis in the world, such experiences are being "gifted" to us "precisely in response to our current needs."

In his clear and comprehensive analysis of others' work on the subject of religion, *Psychology, Religion and Spirituality* (2003), David

Fontana reinforces some of these views: his survey of research on mysticism indicates that mystical experience is in fact relatively common, and that mystics are "notably happier, and notably more free from mental disorders than the norm" (pp. 116-17).

He asserts, too, that mysticism's "most striking feature" is "a sense of unity", described also as a "feeling of all things being one", and that this is found in non-theistic religions such as Buddhism as well as theistic ones. From this he too draws the conclusion that mysticism leads us to feel involved with others rather than just focusing on our own inner life: the sense of union with the divine and/or all creation naturally leads to a feeling of "universal love", of "compassion to all sentient beings" (pp. 123-4).

So mysticism can unite the two strands of individual exploration and the search for unity and community, also potentially uniting exploration across religious divides, and within or outside a religious framework, in that mystical experiences seem to be essentially similar, but are difficult to put into words, or are expressed in poetic images such as "light", "darkness" and "fire", or are described in different words according to the religious or spiritual outlook of the individual mystic. Medieval mystics like Meister Eckhart and the author of *The Cloud of Unknowing* see God as essentially mysterious and unknowable, despite their encounters with the divine in the depths of their being.

Quakerism is very much a mystical religion, from its beginnings rooted in direct experience of the divine, which still forms the basis of our worship and infuses every aspect of our lives. I have heard Meeting for Worship described as an act of "corporate mysticism", bringing us together in unity yet also in freedom, based in silence, with no set words or creeds to divide us. We are known, too, as "practical mystics", seeking to live according to the "leadings" which come to us, both individually and corporately.

Our group of Quaker explorers have shown us that their explorations and discoveries come from their own direct experience, both independently and in community, and extend into their everyday lives. We have seen that other spiritual explorers share with them the desire to explore freely alongside a need for unity and community. And at outreach events we often find enquirers are spiritual explorers too, dissatisfied with institutional religion and wondering if we can give them the spiritual home they are searching for. How might we support them (should they want us to!) to combine free exploration with a sense of belonging?

In some ways, Friends could play a special role at this time. As Damaris Parker-Rhodes puts it: "Quakers are a bridge people… between the past and the future, allowing space for Friends who dare to search within…" (*The way out is the way in*, 1985, quoted in *Quaker Faith and Practice*, 27.44). With our mystical sense of unity and of "that of God in every one", we are open to both traditional and radical views, and can provide a link between them. It seems that our flexible use of religious or spiritual language is particularly helpful: reporting on the 2013 British Quaker Survey, Linda Murgatroyd notes that we are prepared to modify, or translate, our habitual spiritual language, depending on the context, or, presumably, the person or people we are speaking to (The Friend, March 27th 2015). Thus, a Friend I met briefly, at a Woodbrooke Elders' and Overseers' Conference, said she suggested to a Friend in her Local Meeting who was a nontheist, that she substitute a phrase like "the deepest part of myself" for "God.". I would myself see the humanist language of the "Christian atheists" and "Sunday Assembly" members as a reaching towards spirituality, or, as Fontana might put it, a "nontheistic mysticism". Finding a bridge at the other end, with more traditional – particularly evangelical – religion could be more difficult for Friends. Yet even here it seems that connection, if not unity, is possible. Two incidents point the way. Dave, a Bob Dylan fan, once brought along to the writing group a recording made during Dylan's evangelical phase, "Father of day, Father of night", and it was easily possible to translate this anthropomorphic view of God into the mystical sense that God – Spirit – is everywhere, in our darkest as well as our happiest times. And two women Salvation Army officers, who joined a group of us at Woodbrooke for a course on spiritual friendship, spoke a "God-language" very different from ours, yet suggesting a similar sense of deep and close relationship, and in their work for and with people in difficulty they too were "answering that of God in every one."

Ideally, too, our open approach to faith, without set doctrines or hierarchical structures, enables spiritual explorers to find their own pathways among us, well-trodden or still under construction, coming and going as they please, some eventually joining us, others using Quakerism as a starting point or staging post on journeys which will eventually take them elsewhere, yet others as a still, secure point which they are glad to know is there and to which they can return on rare occasions when they feel the need.

But we should not be too self-satisfied. We share some of the difficulties which beset other faith groups, but with added responsibilities since we have no clergy: low numbers, an ageing membership, and members who are "time poor", with heavy family and work commitments. Yet, too often we overburden ourselves with routine business, endless committee meetings, and attempts to find people to fill numerous jobs. Often our over-busyness obstructs our openness to new ideas, and leaves too little time for our essential tasks of worship, reflection and spiritual exploration, social witness and community-building. It is significant that almost all our interviewees are no longer, or have never been, involved in the business side of the Meeting. In Meetings up and down the country, some avoid these commitments; others' energies are drained by them; attenders will not apply for membership in case they are "saddled" with various "jobs". We do need to set our house in order, not because our membership is declining, but because we are depriving some who would feel naturally at home with us of a spiritual home and a chance for further spiritual exploration, of a more fulfilled and enriching life.

There are other reasons why we should not be too complacent: though we do have much to offer, we should not see our Quaker way as superior, for it will not suit everyone. And, at a time of growing religious, racial and nationalist extremism and conflict, and increasing financial and environmental crises, we should not feel that only we have the answers. We need to make common cause with other spiritual explorers and all people of goodwill, of whatever faith or none, to try to begin the process of healing – though our open, "bridging" approach should help us in these tasks. There is still a very long way to go before we can unite in a shared purpose, but my hope is that more and more people may come to realise that our deepest experiences are similar, though expressed in different ways. They are experiences which cut across different traditions and are common to many different times and places: a mystic sense of union with the divine, whatever name we give it, and with our fellow human beings and our home, the Earth, expressed in the compassion which, Karen Armstrong reminds us (in *Twelve Steps to a Compassionate Life*) is a way of being common to all the world's great religions, and potentially to all humanity.

For reflection and sharing

- **What similarities/differences can you see between Quakers and other spiritual explorers?**
- **If you were telling a friend about Quakers, what would you say was best about us? What do you think they would find less acceptable?**
- **If you could reconstruct Quakerism, what changes would you make?**

Suggested Reading

Including books referred to in the text and others which may be of interest

ARMSTRONG, Karen: *The Spiral Staircase* (especially the final chapter), Harper Collins 2004.
Twelve Steps to a Compassionate Life, The Bodley Head 2011

BORG, Marcus: *The Heart of Christianity*, Harper One 2003

BOULTON, David: *Godless for God's Sake: nontheism in contemporary Quakerism*, Dales Historical Monographs 2006

COX, Harvey: *The Future of Faith*, Harper One 2009

DAVIE, Grace: *Religion in Britain since 1945: Believing Without Belonging*, Blackwell 1994

DAWES, Joycelin, Janice DOLLEY and Ike ISAKSEN: *The Quest: exploring a sense of soul: growth and nourishment for your spiritual journey*, O Books 2005

DOLLEY, Janice and Jane OZANNE (eds.). *Awakening to a New Awareness: stories of Contemporary Christians*, CANA Publications 2006 [CANA = Christians Awakening to a New Awareness]

FONTANA, David: *Psychology, Religion and Spirituality*, Blackwell 2003

FORMAN, Robert: *Grassroots Spirituality*, Imprint Academic 2004

HAY, David: *Something There: the biology of the human spirit*, Darton Longman Todd 2006

HICK, John (ed.): *The Myth of God Incarnate*, SCM Press 1977; and author of *The Metaphor of God Incarnate*, SCM Press 2005 (first published 1993)

HOLLOWAY, Richard: *Looking in the Distance: the human search for meaning*, Canongate 2004

JAMES, William, *The Varieties of Religious Experience (Gifford Lectures, 1901-2).* Originally published by Longmans, Green & Co. 1902 – many editions since then, including Penguin Classics 1982, Modern Library (paperback) 1999

JAMIESON, Alan: *A Churchless Faith: Faith Journeys beyond the Churches*, SPCK 2002

JARMAN, Roswitha, *Breakthrough to Unity: the Quaker Way held within the mystic traditions*, The Kindlers 2010

LEONARD, Alison: *Living in Godless Times: Tales of Spiritual Travellers*, Floris Books, 2001; *Telling our Stories*, Darton Longman Todd, 1995

LYNCH, Gordon: *The New Spirituality: an introduction to progressive belief in the 21st century*, IB Tauris, 2007

MOONEY, Bel: *Devout Sceptics*, Hodder & Stoughton, 2003

MOUNTFORD, Brian: *Christian Atheist: belonging without believing*, O Books 2011

NOLAN, Albert: *Jesus before Christianity: the Gospel of Liberation*, DLT 1977

ROBINSON, John A.T.: *Honest to God*, SCM Press 1963

SKIDMORE, Gil: *Turning Inside Out; an exploration of spiritual autobiography*, Sowle Press 1996

SPONG, John Shelby: *Why Christianity Must Change or Die*, Harper San Francisco 1998

TACEY, David: *The Spirituality Revolution: our changing perception of the ultimate mystery*, Brunner-Routledge 2004 (first published by Harper Collins Sydney, Australia 2001)

TILLICH, Paul: *The Shaking of the Foundations*, Penguin Books 1962 (first published 1949).

Acknowledgements

Special thanks go to the interviewees, for their willingness to share their stories with me and with readers of this booklet.

But spiritual insights, inspiration and support have come to me from many different directions: from my late husband, Martin, and other members of my family, and from Quakers near and far: other members of the writing group, Friends in my present and former Meetings, in my Experiment with Light group and from my Quaker Retreat Group days, not forgetting Ffriends and acquaintances encountered elsewhere, often at Quaker gatherings, particularly at Woodbrooke Quaker Study Centre. Kindlers' courses, both at Woodbrooke and "on-the-Road", along with their booklets, have given me fresh inspiration.

"New light" has come, too, from non-Quaker friends old and new, some met at retreats/quiet days and conferences. Courses run by my Ffriend Brenda, at the "small local retreat house" mentioned several times in *Explorations*, attended by people from a variety of religious/spiritual backgrounds, have provided a rich source of reflection.

And of course there have been so many inspirational writers, speakers and radio and television presenters, only some of whom can be mentioned in this booklet. Particular thanks are due to the writers of Woodbrooke's distance learning courses, especially *Gifts and Discoveries* and *Becoming Friends*; and to Eley McAinsh of the Living Spirituality Network, for her reflections on contemporary spirituality and mysticism, briefly discussed in Chapter 5.

All of you have played your part in creating *Explorations* – my heartfelt thanks to you all.

Judith